Love and I

Also by Fanny Howe

Poetry

Eggs
Poem from a Single Pallet
Robeson Street
The Vineyard
Introduction to the World
The Quietist
The End
O'Clock
One Crossed Out
Selected Poems
Gone
Tis of Thee
On the Ground
The Lyrics
Come and See
Second Childhood

Fiction

Forty Whacks
First Marriage
Bronte Wilde
Holy Smoke
In the Middle of Nowhere
The Deep North
Famous Questions
Saving History
Nod
Indivisible
Economics
Radical Love: Five Novels
The Lives of a Spirit / Glasstown: Where Something Got Broken
What Did I Do Wrong?
The Wages

Essays

The Wedding Dress: Meditations on Word and Life
The Winter Sun: Notes on a Vocation
The Needle's Eye: Passing through Youth

Love and I

POEMS

Fanny Howe

Graywolf Press

This publication is made possible, in part, by the voters of Minnesota through a Minnesota State Arts Board Operating Support grant, thanks to a legislative appropriation from the arts and cultural heritage fund. Significant support has also been provided by Target, the McKnight Foundation, the Lannan Foundation, the Amazon Literary Partnership, and other generous contributions from foundations, corporations, and individuals. To these organizations and individuals we offer our heartfelt thanks.

Published by Graywolf Press
250 Third Avenue North, Suite 600
Minneapolis, Minnesota 55401

www.graywolfpress.org

Published in the United States of America

ISBN 978-1-64445-004-8

2 4 6 8 9 7 5 3 1
First Graywolf Printing, 2019

Library of Congress Control Number: 2019931351

Cover design: Kyle G. Hunter

Cover art: Colleen McCallion, *Beyond* (painting)

Love that never told can be

—William Blake

Love and I

Allegories

I love so many of them
But they are only half a decade
Away from being disproved.
Remnants themselves already
Like polar-wolves
From the vortex.
It could be a nuclear site
But it's just a bar
With the bottles going dark
For the soldiers without uniforms.

Its last model is reproduction.

Is love one-way?

Almost always
It catches on a kiss.
Holds still for a flash.

1941

On a cold day near Lake Erie
I was in a double bind.
The snow was like a lamb
Shorn in the upper circle.

Someone pushed me over the ice and stones.
Someone else chattered behind.
A rubber nipple was pressed on my lips.
Gagged and spat until my tears were milk.

Everything seemed like something else.

The number of wheels was too large
For my body to contain in a dream.
But the silver bar could be seen to be long
With faces beaming in reflection

From the land of the living.
I thought I saw a flock impaled on a fence
Then more clouds, god-free, overhead.
Zero and One sat on either side of me.

Was trapped in apparatus and a family
Like so many before and after.
A central contradiction, once discovered,
Leads to collapse or evolution.

The tremors in the heavens
Created weather. We all mentioned this
For years when we met
On our quest for happiness.

Turbulence

Some who never feel loved keep traveling.

They sense that an airplane will change their fate
By separating them from gravity.

They say goodbye to air and pebbles when boarding.
Strapped down
They must go on living because they have scores to settle.

And when the wings tremble, suddenly they love to talk to God.

Chatter like I tell you:
"Thank you for the candle colors folding inside the wax."

I loved the shadow and being away from shouting girls at school.
This went on at a lowering frequency.

There was rain on the porthole of the plane
because rain rains sideways
on a tipped wing.

The clouds were below with the puzzle of the past.
Bits of world clicked into place.

The wrong God saw this and showed no humor.
Instead tears rained down on Iran.

Then slowly and as usual the left God turned
Into a luminous eye.
Blue more blind than white.

Both you and the passenger beside you
Were two no God would never see again
In any sense as faithfully as then.

One has perseverance but is full of fear.
Another has no perseverance but is brave.

Which one would you rather sit beside?
"My stamina isn't up to either.

My brain is like the sun I can't look at.
Or like a slave still tired in his grave."

Devils stroll with angels into our daily lives
But we don't know who is which until it's too late.

"From burned forest to subway hole,
what can't I recognize but must?"

Your cosmology is an impossible tangle
of planets and stars crashing into each other.

"Strands, yes, of fine colors, that glorified eyesight
and the ability to recognize . . . a dangerous trust."

The sky hurts
My eyes at noon.
Snow shelves
The oval porthole:
Inside is gray.
Gems gild the
Crusted ice
That no one can see.

A man might not want a child
Because he has his brain to carry around.

The passenger who whispered
Clutched his head like an infant.

I understood him.

He was sick of pontificating over revisions and drafts
Until they ruined the first burst.

This is how he explained it to me.
A solitary wreck winking back tears:

"I was scared, scared of leaving my dreams behind
and no one to interpret them."

When dawn mingles with air, things begin to take form as
    planes and spheres.
They might start as clouds of stars or rain or gods or spurts
    of water.
Soon the filmy forms take an animal turn.
Androgynous. Emotive. We may never really know
Since now we see through lenses and probes.

Druids could not separate what they saw around them from
    their thoughts.
Clouds were struggling to become gods.

Twigs and snow-prints were their words.

Nature was the name for everything that moved.
Nature was consciousness.

Poor universe. Self-sufficient. Nothing can be added.
    Only returned.

Give up your wires, plugs, laptop, pills, water, cellphone,
     passport, ticket and shoes.
Give up your water, your wine, your songs and stories.
Put your arms up, your feet down flat and face ahead.

You have not reached the end yet.

"What degradation to be thinking how to OD
technically, infallibly, by choice.
To expect an answer to: Now?

Soon we will be standing in line with each other
at a relocation center
as if we wanted to be there where the meek
left their hiding places."

Now the wing is whitening, its patches quiver
On the steel and fragment into petals that are either living
     or not.
In grade one I watched the lights of cars passing on the
     bedroom wall
For surely they were messages flying at the speed of light.
And aren't they still?

In the air there are few signs of progress.
Tongues wag and sailors pull their beards.
Some have pictures of naked women, some have boys.

Pebbles like minced bones under seventy-degree sunshine.
It's this place part symbolic of something you never met.

Each raindrop on the wingspan
Pierces the drop beside it and all the way to

Where there is no one left.
Flight is an underused option on an airplane.

The center that runs along the sides of the tarmac
Is a camp without a name.
A holding station.

A glass of narcotics, a warm blanket, steam for suffocation
For each passenger of any class.

"Did you know a rendition is an interpretation, an
explanation of something not clear?"

"It's also persecution and surrender,
translation and the handing over
of prisoners to countries
where detention is."

Pass through customs in silence.
The red strings of radiation
Will only burn your bed-skins.
Do not joke or rhyme with bomb.

"If you have a passport, bless it."

No Beginning

Stop in your tracks.
Take off your shoes.
Close your eyes.
The Word knows what to do.

For the blind, touching is seeing.

Home?
In.

The Word is like a flood in shape and speed.
You will like the way it rushes east and west at the same time.

Echoes and solidifies and breaks apart.
It streams like a Northern Light. But it's the Word.

The Word makes no sound.
The Word never made no sound and will not
Ever, out of parched minds and tongues
Break this law.

The Word is not particles or waves or tangles.
It runs all around.

The Word wrote itself and continues to write.

Stuffs the papyrus away in space.
Invisible ink and yet it runs.

It runs ahead of the mouth of the west.
It meets itself running the other way.

If you want to appear, turn to another.

The Word lives alone everywhere
Lives as a pariah
That attentive
Listeners will know by ear.

The Word doth say and attend
Only to this sad refrain:

"Listen. We did our best."

Our lives were saved, it wasn't fair.
We had to let the animals die.
The second to last came at dawn. He shoveled
Up the roots and burned them.
There were about one hundred boots from the soldiers who
    died in Iraq.
Dirty and curled at the toes.

What should we do? What can we do? Take off your shoes.

You've walked far enough.

Take them off and feel the ground.
You've come a long way against the sun.

What's about to come?

Crusty desert, stone-grown towns, barefoot children,
Not even a crown of thorns. Salt rivers.
Snow-white animals dipping into foam
New ideas for different things.

We don't have a name for God.
But the Word still holds.

Will we row across a rubbery sea
Or bob in the sky
Vomiting, singing, falling over
Losing our voices, our wits, our hearing?

Will our lives have meaning?

"No meaning" means
There's no big bang, no beginning.

If a shoe is lying on a highway
It indicates an accident.

When two shoes are crossed
It means instability.

When two shoes are lined up
It means a door.

You will never see the face
But can guess the age.

Sneak away!
The race is ending.

There might be a brighter night
When fires turn black and we disappear.

Always hold both east and west
And be sure to wear two shoes.

Put your feet on the ground, Moses.
Take off your hood.

And what's that in your hand?

My staff.

Your coat?

The sheep enjoy the smell.

Take it off.
And throw it in the bin.

Everything human is poisoned.
You must burn, not bury one.

In a man-made world
You can't buy wood.

Monastic Life

Love stayed beside me
So never spoke a word.
Sister Death was silent too.
Both heavy as trees
Or light depending
On the clouds above.

When love became a face
Down the wind blowing
With the street
Asking where you went
We were frightened
We couldn't tell them apart.

By allegory go
Across the map
A ladybug on a block
Red hot, black spot.

Say every page
Was once a leaf.

The allegory is this:
Paper, skin and blood
Feel the feet
Of least weight.

Gentle tender
Pricks of thorn and ink
Blue vein rivers
In a wrist weathering.

Monostich: a long sentence
Sternum: a little chest
Heart: upside down

Location of the unconscious:
Empty window seat

Horizon: gone at night
Thought: given
Prison: a perversion

Our earth can't live without holy rites.
You can see this from the sky.

Lots of hills to climb up and down.
A straight ravine between.

Snow figures engraved in stones.
Show streaks of sun gone but
The white rocks shrink and grow
Grave at sunset.

Turn to the right
And you will fall to the left.

One figure wears a beard
Down to his chest

But Eros hates coverings.
And prefers to be caught naked

With his bow and arrow.

Embellishes
But clears the way for pathos.

From above I covet a mountain beneath my feet.

Shrines made of dung and branches
With berries for eyes and burlap hung with holly.
They were curled in shadows on roads
Leading to every stop we made from the Trig

To Top Withens to Liverpool.
The white and purple mountains.
Stood over the Brontës and clusters
Of black thistles script.

I remember a church (a cave supported
By old bicycle parts to keep it up)
Was bound by a broken bell and a box
Containing snapshots and trinkets.

"We will get through this!"

Why mercy?

Having mercy on someone is easier than forgiving them.

That one there?

A man limited by logic, he imprisoned the people whose
thinking was infinite.

And her, the serious one?

Stars without light hold the others up.

I lost you for a moment.

Mid-sentence is darker so you can't decipher it.
Look up.

Oyster, shell pink, sky inside. Our prison.

What would you tell the judge?

The difference between a man who shoots others and then
himself and
one who shoots others and runs away.

You will tell her that decisions are only guesses.
"I wish they would shoot themselves before they shoot the
others."
"Murder is a weak form of suicide."

That's why suicide is hard to choose even when you're dying.

Time was vertical. Is, and past perfect.

A monastic said she loves to live alone
In a turret with a weed garden.
I prefer a pod while she likes hives.
We confess we both wear armor
Outside our habitats.

Water was our first armor before our skin.
Then came the bristle of sunshine
And a thickening of blood into oil
Or syrup in the lower veins.
Covering up our prototypes.

Everything we saw, we became.
This was before the buildings.
The subways, the tracks. I think
All life loved itself—
The weakest especially.

What if the outcome of an act burst into color.
All that fruit skin dimpled from the touch of branches.
The oranges falling when the creatures below were hungry.

What if every living part of the created world
Lifted itself up to help the next part.
What if you stood when I entered.

What if you think of time as a long and everlasting plain,
You can pass across it any which way you turn.
And walk around the pond with your father time and again.

Mysteries

I had a garden of my own
For twenty-one years.
Seven trees times three
Planted for the first children.

On its land was a meadow
And our little house, a grape arbor
And a Wampanoag
Grave in a grove of elms.

Then a tree like an elephant
Bucked in a storm.
And its trunk broke into
A wrinkled little stump.

Roots don't give up.

And stones only breathe once a year.

Many people passed through.
We could have watered more
Or flowered a path
For the visitors. After all

Love was a law.
Children played and grew.
I too grew old for no reason.
Love stood at a distance.

One day the snow will camouflage
The huddling April buds
Before a cherry picker
Damns all but one, the littlest.

At least I know when the wild geese
Fly from Sepiessa
They herd the future
As it approaches the bench.

Night . . . the playground
At Town Hall is creaking
And tribal members
Now numbered

In the twos are too early for sunup.

We almost sit together
But our feet of shadows
Show failed land deals.
Steps lowered and slimy

On a slip into the lagoon.
Ghoulish are the ghosts
Of time past: ancestors
With our same names.

Pensées sauvages: wild pansies, like violets, have the shape of
thoughts, savage thoughts, colored thoughts, sprung from
a stem.

Purple and yellow. Five petals.

Once Cupid shot an arrow dipped in the ink of a pansy onto
the eyelid of a sleeping child.

From then on the child saw cirrus colors at dawn—dawn.

1995

We were at an oblong table
Ending with poppy seed cake
And sweet German wine.

It was fifty years after the extermination
And we were laughing
And speaking of life-spans.

What a perfect sight but none of the actual
Persons remain. Since that night

I've sensed there was always someone else
Everywhere I went, even
On nights unparalleled.

2016

Rain never came
Though it was December
And the pond was full.
And the philosopher had a fire going.
We ate around a round table.
Thick potato soup
Then chicken curry.
Mince pies and chocolates.
A glass of red and water.
So what's your future going to be?
The grown-ups asked us.
Adventure, poetry, Italy,
Ministry, decrepitude, queer
Wishes to be effective.
Then the piano and song.

Was sleeping all this time.
Down with the fallen.
And rusty leaves were blowing
And garbage bins rolling.
Everywhere we went, even
For hours with friends,
We each slept alone.

2011

On the last bus from Dublin to Limerick
Raindrops pelted the landscape
And held little photos
Of aluminum crutches in each drop
Rolling down the glass.
These were buildings built
On phony loans that bankrupted
The country. Pharmaceuticals
And cheap hospital
Industry styles and ghost estates.
There were only two people on the bus
Plus the driver and a baby
In a cradle shaped like a quiver.
Everywhere I look, my thoughts grow wild.

Philophany

The clatter of rain has a personal meaning.
This is the time to meditate or write down your dreams.
But the lover can do neither, can only wander
From room to room trying not to spill what's so precious.

Around the lover are myriad sounds.
Thoughts shine through like water.
Forms, shapes, colors, stations are glorified in the morning.
Indecipherable, almost transparent.

Fear of loss takes root in the blood of the lover.
Words form, interpretations.

Miracles: no one there where someone was.
Someone here where no one was.

The stars that shine are sparks and coal
As if to show experience purifies existence.

Experience was everything to me.
(This is what the uneducated would say.)

Every word must come from my acts direct.
But I know the difficulty too.
Who will believe what I do?

Night Philosophy

Night philosophy becomes theology:
We've not seen such darkness for centuries.

Every thought condensed into a death before dying.
Then a shout: *who?*

So you believe in predestination?

Sometimes.

I remember a child who licked up the mist on the
windowpane to see eternity.

One boy has a bomb strapped to his chest and another rides
his skateboard through the traffic.

On a snowy Christmas there was a pause between each sixth
gong of the bell.

A sun that looked like nine but it was already noon: is when?

Red raspberries turned black on that same path. I recall frost
around the nipple.

What is your faith?

Crack anything and you will let free the spirit of liberty.

The open red throat of a sick child.

It's as if words are remnants of thoughts that can't be caught.

I never heard such faith in my childhood house.

Why did the names of seasons depress me that year?
I was near the end but not there
And would have been a lot happier if I had not said "summer"
When I was talking to a friend.

The wind was shaking the blinds
Onto the blue of Massachusetts Bay.
Was stricken at the word "summer."
As if I could go to the island and return to
A time not a season.

I still believed my love is standing here.

Black Mountain Boston

First there is a minimum house
And then a quiet house.
Katherine Litz has her back to the dining hall,
Her foot extended and looks at the lake and the Black Mountain.
And Charles Olson sits beside a window.
Anni Albers draws knots
And John Dewey the Democrat
Weaves thought into matter.

These are their relics.
They have fabrics hanging in space
And lines of music without notes.
This is why they stand by a door like those
Who choose an aisle seat.
They have left these traces
Of their silence, neuroses and histories
(Their pots and dishes and textiles
Open to air.)

They are a proud and poetic people.
You can tell. They can't be forced
To stay anywhere but never stay still.
They don't say die, they say disappear.

————

A transparent leaf.

A piano where leaves of music flutter.

One of them could uncover and reproduce the pattern
Of a kitten's coat by using string
Of various colors, pulled tight.
Before the fur has grown in.

Look at their faces. Anni Albers has seen everything.
John Cage has not and still has hope.
John Dewey is analytical but his mouth is soft.

Dewey noticed life is education enough.
Can you teach life?
Yes, experiment.

So what is the teacher's purpose except
To offer a space for failure?

Dewey said, "We get used to the chains we wear."

A free-hanging space divider,
Knots of wool and string uncurling,
Mirrors of stars and plasma from their brains
That have evolved at the same rate as Einstein's.

Ancient people drew glyphs and Katherine Litz
In a bag choreographed one.
Merce Cunningham made an alphabet out of his arms and legs.

The mathematical genius of the glyph-carvers
Shows that time is not progress.

Depth gets you somewhere you recognize.

Maybe you find what you knew already.

⸺

Josef Albers taught in America without the English language.
Paint and proportion were his vocabulary.
It was the Weimar period in Germany
Bauhaus had ended under the aesthetic of Hitler.
Painters painted in abstractions and codes.

⸺

Dewey noted that it takes a lot of work
To change a person's beliefs.
He dared them to try.

Outside the window of the Black Mountain show
Boston had the russet and reserved tone
Of the nineteenth century.
Trees like devotees of the sea bowed down
To a rocky shoreline.

The experimental arts don't thrive in this city
Being unteachable.

⸺

Some unteachables are children, some are poems.
Some poets remain children.

Why write what can't be taught?

Alice Coltrane drove her shuttle out of her saxophone.
An octave or a fifth, it was her inner god having fun.

Sun Ra was her friend.

I wanted to go to their planet with them.
But she said, "You have to be tough to live the spiritual life."

2000

The ordeal of dying must be memory, so much seeing and
    losing forms.
Friends whacking at invisible ankles and you.

The action is done in a dream. Who did what? The closed
    book, the feet asleep.

Proof that you lived is that you kept notebooks.

Are you collecting material for dreams, she asked the audience.

None of them remembered collecting or dreaming.
Nothing specific, that is.

For a book, no.

They lay down that night not looking for a real thing but for
    a way back.
A dream broke time apart.

You're allowed to fear the coming hallucinations, she added.

Destinations

You met me at the subway
Where tracks led east to
North Station and on
Up to Cape Ann.

We were almost romantic
Not knotted but erect
Side by side passively waiting
For an apocalyptic collision to rupture

The grave tension between wholly conscious
Ontological thinking
And the steel pebbling motion of tracks
Sparked into action by a fiery touch.

We smiled our way forward perfectly even.

In a faraway land
And a hotel I never visited.
There were ninety-nine hells
In a ghost book half-erased.

Like this I was in love with a non-entity.
This was the hardest part assigned to me.
During my brief tenure I loved loving best
One who didn't exist.

In the early days, it was the opposite.
Nature (even mine)
Did exist and loved itself.
Clouds doted on the sea, amorousness

Was in the air returning every wave and sigh.
The squirrels told the oak
To shake its acorns down
For the dirt to eat.

I almost touched you

On a Saturday

The wind blew easterly.
There was a jar of mums
On a table near the window.

Their yellows were calling
To each other.

Place-names
Were put back
In the pencil drawer
Before I saw
Your shadow.

First the sky was too close
then white snow followed.

On a hand
was an amethyst: a cube of lilac in hospital light.

Whose fault is it when no one visits?

Last night I dreamed
I was in a peaceful place
but woke up
freezing and ashamed.

On a side street (on my sheets)
one I loved passed
as a shadow.
Maddish, reddish, his fist
clenched for a fight.

I recalled
his body color
being soft like a child.

Honey I called
We were too late.

You—like a dwarf-lover
of a giant-killer
crouched in the nave.

Would do anything
to become something new.
Scientists asked why
You had to hide away
With the ruins of religion.

To take the weight off your feet?

To look at stained glass windows
Sort of honey like a waffle cone
With sweet cream and berries inside.

The tinier the beauty the better.
A bird's cherry-pit heart pulsed between two bones.

There's a softening
To the bricks outside
And the thousand-mile storm
Is leaving where it's coming from:
From the long ago to my abode.

I'll sit at the window
Where it's safe to say no.
Won't go out, won't work
For a living, will study the clouds
Becoming snow.

Not with a spyglass
But with a wild guess
And only three words: "You never know."
Now I see others like me
Thinning into the least thing.

Downstairs, cries of lust.
Up here, a requiem mass
And light to lead the clouds home
To the past.

Back Bay Station is waiting for you to return.
Two terrible times: one without a kiss of greeting
And one with her running to give you the bad news.
The bad news of failure and public humiliation.
Back Bay Station is waiting for you to turn and give
the blessing.
At last: every trace of that hour is gone.

To be described as a note that separates from a song and
blows away.

When you are down to nothing more to call on.

You can say I walked Manhattan from sundown to dawn.
"So I *have* traveled the world."

In London you stepped over crypts and dungeons to see a
film starring friends—
Americans.
The ceiling collapsed from heavy rain and artificial colors
condensed along the sidewalk.

Time had thinned for gravity and a spinning reel
Since time was lightweight and round.

Someone help me find an animal
Who will rescue me from
Being a solitary
And more like my friends the wrens
In an evergreen shrub: to be clear
Would be wonderful.
A sigh without the ghostly gasps
That accompany passion.
Still I do desire more
Of the kind no one can see or hear.
Not that second, rasping sigh of success.
Find me instead
More like the breathy Saint Bernard.
But a little dog.
A cask of brandy hanging at her neck.

Primrose for X

I was tracking Blake on Primrose Hill
one damp summer night.
Bundles of white chestnut flared
under the streetlights.

London's unsteady skyline
was not a reassuring one
but like a graph that measures
markets, snails and heartbeats.

When one brain was weary
one heart was not.
The brain can be shucked
when all the air is gone but the heart

is slippery and needs a touch of
spirit to nourish it.
How am I still here
at every thump?

The heart has its needs
and feelings sewn like threads
into branches and seasons
that we pencil as trees.

The Irish women with brass-capped hair
and tight mouths
and a Muslim woman with five girls and one boy
are all sadly clad at Victoria.

In poverty some screaming brats
are fat, and some are starved
into silence on their father's laps.
No father might be worse than that.

What is created by humans
is almost always alien.
The hissing buses and trains
in Kentish Town, boys hunched

in bunches on the lock
drugged and dirty and crushed
their eyes like lizards veiled
and blind in retreat while

a man with a machete
cut a fellow down, blood
all over his hands. Proud
of being a killing kind of man.

Machete or his father's hand: which one
caused this crime?
The aughts were grievous years
for boys and men.

Crowds of phantoms covered
Kent's fields as the Eurostar
raced away from London
and Blake's theophanies.

The First Church

One dawn I crawled out of the gutter
Into the Common: just a woman in tears.

A group of children was snoozing nearby.
Don't wake us up!
They cried as if they were half-alive.

I kneeled on my rug and swatted the air.
Sandwiches and small canteens were spilled nearby.

Flies delivering maggots gathered around.

I hate buzzing sounds I said to the kids.
Shut up, a little boy cried, I'm dreaming.

Where is the child I came here to save?

Is it that little slave they made in the lab?

A creature created to be put to work at once.
It has no feelings, just what they want.

In the end they threw it in the sewer
Like the tin soldier who had no passport.

Then the boys and girls lift
Their arms over their heads:

(*Hands up! Don't shoot!*)

And the day has only four words we can believe.

Neon clothes hangers brighten the laundromat.

One boy naps face up on a bench.
A gold badge shines above his head,

Another lies on the floor at Juvenile Hall.
The kids wish a crocus would grow on the linoleum.

Children need a rest, their minds are swimming in junk
    and fists.
They want the water of the unconscious.
It would mean childhood more or less.

Look at them sprawled where George Washington stood,
Their backpacks like skunks curled in the shade.

Some kids concentrate
On plastic and metal
As if on threads and a red
Pin cushion, the snow
Falling like pepper
On the tar outside.
The letters in color
That have messages
Stuck to each other.

Listening to hip-hop
With their keypads clicking
They pierce the veils
Of material
To see the other side.

They're practicing transcendence.

The boy wears a burlap tunic
Designed by Francis of Assisi.
In Limerick an artist preserves it
In a reliquary with a handle.

One child is as poor as genocide
And needs to be buried
When the gold diggers of the world
Are stalking the cliffs and caves

Of the cities. They want to measure him
Buried in trash! He is folded
Into a black plastic bag:
What is one life worth without money?

This is the question of the century.

They moved from pillow to bench.

One sees her old calendar has a tartan pattern.

I, little Eugenia, have written about this, but the writing was
    discarded even as it appeared.
It was a miracle: to produce what disappeared.

Next it was a molecule she was asked to accept as the measure
    of her life. That wasn't difficult.

A cloud was already being prepared.

So we all fell asleep that afternoon
Like drunks on a picnic.

Nobody jerked us from our confusion.
Not pilgrims or immigrants or angels from another field.

Sun on closed lids inspires illusions.

When I was a girl there was an orange pearl
That turned the butter yellow
With four strokes of a wooden spoon.

A dirty girl had her own sunbeam that stayed by her side

When she stood on her head.
All lifelong it was the beam assigned to her.

A bolt, a thread, and shining honor.
Sometimes it covered her like a shawl, sometimes
It lay down with her shadow,
Sometimes it sat by her side, protectively, and

Other times it sparkled in her hair like an aura.

Footsore, feet that can't fit
Into your sister's shoes anymore.

Go on then, give them to the poorer!
Time is stacked in layers.

Everything created is still here
Alive without, but hiding.

She laid out a patch of grass
As an offering to the inevitable.
Woven of vetch, pinks, a gentian and a daisy
It showed her family loafing.
And had a brown dog watching.

(My friend before dying gave me a flower
That never needed water.)
She always needed water.

The shrub was still there by the back door
Of the house and all the trees were present.
This is the past I can give you
As you fly ascendant by

But most importantly please visit her
And soothe those you created now in agony.

I keep hearing about a magic cloak
On a spreading horizon
Where one shake changes earth's direction
Across the warp of time.
Web-elastic eternally speaking
Pinched by streaks.

This cloak protects you in the dark.
Children come here.
Here, closer to my yarn.
I know about each of each.
But I must be missing a piece.
They're too much alike to pull apart.

Children need sugar.
Especially in danger.
A thumb and finger
Can go numb.

Any sugar will save them.
It can be brown white or yellow.
Press it on their tongue
Or help them steal some.

Elderberry jam and honey?
Cloud berries soaked in brandy?
Golden jelly, sugar cane
For one little law-breaker.

Pepper spray brings tears
pain and temporary blindness.

It's made of the fruit of plants and chilies
ground into powder by a pestle
and soaked in ethanol.

That spray is the way it feels
to be violated by your guards
Sharp and hard.
Like rock salt drying the skin
on your back
and them humming
"I am your experience."

A lot of boys and girls were forced from home.

They're at rest at last.
They were transported by wood on the sea.

Look at them!

I wish I could see a day when we
Had our own acre and shared the guitar
But I'm only hoping so don't make me swear.

They walked the moat.
Brown grasses pansies roses white clematis and hellebore.
Glad to live below and have mercy and no power.

They would crawl backwards rather than climb up to the tower.

We were near the First Church of Christ
At the hour the city hall
Creaks with adolescent tramps:

Boys and girls you can pity
Mercilessly. Pimples
And rings in their tongues and noses.

They snore and shake and flip
From psychosis back into religion.

One was glad God stayed in outer space.

Another one wanted God in the ground but breathing.

One was hopeful that God moved around handing things out.

There is a wonderful kidnapped hunted raped and
    betrayed girl
In fairy tales. She has a name, but the vowels and subjects
Can't be switched to fit.

She wants to escape, but letters won't let her.

She never thinks about darkness or dying because they're
    natural
And don't require thought.

She covers her head with a crown and a hoodie.
"You never know" is her mantra.

If only clay could walk
If only clay could talk
And its legs climb up!
If it could stay gray

And stick its hands together
And pull them apart
Without a snap,
Then take a breath?

Would that be will power?

When dry in every cranny.
When wettened
And breathed into
Out of its soft cunning

Will there be a full
Cup of desire
A discovery
Like Adam's first orgasm?

The clay figure lives
For form
First distorted—climbs
Around brains

Squeezed and gray,
Insensate like
A bone or decree.
We don't know what to do with it.

Many mothers I loved
Walked the underworld
To find their children
Sleeping under a ramp.
Canals and cans, urinals and sandals
Broken boys & girls
With studs in their tongues.
We wept away the hours
While the police combed the streets
With surveillance and guns.
Mothers carried in their pockets
Ear buds, candy bars and bread.

Get up and stand on your feet!

Go build an altar.
Not just a stage but with all of you
Eating and playing
Airplanes and dolls, butter
From bread on your fingertips.
Why are you crying?
Why are your eyes shut?
Let's shake up a rhythm
And scuff the dust on asphalt.

Get up, get up!

Up stood a child, dirty and loud, and her boots furry.
An immigrant from the United States.

She went everywhere with me, this disgrace with no money.

She had the pallor of—say
Someone who never passed through the God phase.

Silvery gray is its weather.

Soft char rubbed off a gun barrel or an eyelid.
She didn't want others to see the way she saw herself.

Roast lamb. Mint jelly.

Sprigs scenting the meat like incense.

A burnt offering is the only one
That love has pity for.

Not rare or well done.

But burned, burned, burned.

The Lamb

The plurality of the apple
makes us dare to pulp.
Can we breed lambs
without seeing meat?

This is my body
I cannot eat.

Once the lambs
were tender toward the shepherd.

Now they shall want
to take his eyes off them.

Lamb unremembered so many
hanging and days spent fenced in.

Split lips for laughter to be released or songs
or bleats, memories ejected onto canvas or score
or brains where they burned
their impressions in.

Spray, dispersion, atoms, up close for crying.
They had no bleat without a mother to create and hear it.

Not the lamb—

its fleece, eyes, meat, tongue, heart
are tied up for a factory.

At first there were folds.
Now there are millions of mass-produced

bundles of wool:
wrapped on hooks for the fridge and the loom.

My shepherd's a figure
Invisible to all.
The sheep little siblings
Of no harm done.

Bridal curls
Pre-cotton in the clover.
A smile without content.
Pink and sweet.

From meadow to meadow
Eternal grass.
My shepherd of the flock
Stay close.

(I can't breathe.)

Wherever
You go twice is blessed.

Index

Acknowledgments

Thanks to *Arts & Letters*, *Bomb*, *Brick*, *Conjunctions*, *Golden Handcuffs*, Heroes Are Gang Leaders, *Poetry*, Song Cave, and *Vallum* for their kind acceptance of my poems. Thanks, as always, to the staff at Graywolf, especially to my careful and caring editor, Jeff Shotts.

Fanny Howe is the author of many books of poetry and prose, including *The Needle's Eye: Passing through Youth*, *The Winter Sun: Notes on a Vocation*, *The Wedding Dress: Meditations on Word and Life*, and *Radical Love: Five Novels*. Her most recent collection of poetry, *Second Childhood*, was a finalist for the 2014 National Book Award. Her work in fiction was recognized as a finalist for the 2015 Man Booker International Prize. She received the 2009 Ruth Lilly Poetry Prize from the Poetry Foundation for lifetime achievement, and she has won the Lenore Marshall Poetry Prize from the Academy of American Poets and the Gold Medal for Poetry from the Commonwealth Club of California. She lives in New England.

The text of *Love and I* is set in Adobe Garamond Pro.
Book design by Rachel Holscher. Composition by Bookmobile
Design and Digital Publisher Services, Minneapolis, Minnesota.
Manufactured by Versa Press on acid-free,
30 percent postconsumer wastepaper.